What to do
when your mom or dad says...
"WE CAN'T AFFORD IT!"

By
JOY WILT BERRY

Living Skills Press
Fallbrook, California

Distributed by:

Word, Incorporated
4800 W. Waco Drive
Waco, TX 76710

Dear Parents,

How often are you forced to respond to your children's request for money with the words, **"WE CAN'T AFFORD IT!"**? Financial responsibility rests with the parents. But children can be allowed to assume some responsibility for family finances when they understand the basics of household economics. This book explains family finances in simple terms so that children can understand what it means when a parent says, **"WE CAN'T AFFORD IT!"**

A family's financial situation is often a result of circumstances beyond its control. Nevertheless, financial trouble can make parents feel guilty and angry. The pressures of economic problems can divide a family by virtue of the strong emotions attached to money and its role in the family lifestyle.

When children lack an understanding of their family's finances, their reactions to the words **"WE CAN'T AFFORD IT!"** are often negative. These feelings can result in negative behavior like complaining, nagging, threatening and badgering. Such negative feelings and behavior do not serve to improve the family's financial situation.

Understanding brings about acceptance of the realities of family finances and promotes a united effort aimed at improving the situation. Children have a role to play in family economics because of the expense of their needs and wants. With information and understanding, the role can be expanded to include contributions to the family income. Children's support of the family's financial plan plays a vital role in freeing adult energies, which can then be applied to earning more money for the family.

WE CAN'T AFFORD IT! defines income, details expenses, and explains the possible reasons for a loss of income. Children learn that there are six things they can do to help when family finances are in trouble:

1. Be understanding.
2. Be helpful.
3. Be careful, not wasteful.
4. Stop careless spending.
5. Earn money when possible.
6. Get involved in the family finances.

Children need to know about things that have a direct effect on their lives. Family finances directly affect nearly every facet of children's lives, yet children often feel ignorant of the facts and helpless to do anything. In **WE CAN'T AFFORD IT!** children learn to become part of the solution instead of part of the problem.

This process can be encouraged by a game which uses the family's monthly income in the form of play money and the family's expenses in bills due. This clear demonstration of income and expenses promotes family discussion and united efforts to solve the family's financial problems. With your children's understanding and help, you may never again have to say, **"WE CAN'T AFFORD IT!"**

Sincerely,

Joy Wilt Berry

4

Has your mother or father ever told you . . .

When your parents tell you that they cannot afford to buy you something, do you ever wonder...

If any of this sounds familiar to you, you are going to **love** this book.

Because it will explain why your parents may not be able to afford something and what you can do about it.

Every family has an **INCOME**.

An income is the money that a family receives.

There are several ways a family gathers income.

1. Family members work and get paid for their work.
2. Family members sell things that they own.
3. Interest is earned or profits are made on money that has been saved or invested.
4. Someone outside the family gives family members money, such as a gift or an inheritance.

Every family has **EXPENSES.**

Expenses are the things that a family spends its money on.

Most family expenses include:

- food
- shelter (house, trailer, or apartment)
- utilities (water, gas, electricity, or garbage collection)
- telephone
- transportation (car expenses; bus or train fare)
- clothing
- medical bills (doctor, dentist, or orthodontist)
- taxes
- insurance
- repairs (on house, car, or equipment)
- child care and education
- donations
- entertainment (hobbies, outings, or vacations)
- miscellaneous (such as gifts)

11

A family's financial situation is all right when its *income is equal to its expenses*. When the money a family receives is the same as the money it spends, the family will have enough money for what it needs and wants.

A family's situation is even better when its *income is greater than its expenses.* When the money a family receives is more than the money it spends, the family will have extra money after it has paid for what it needs and wants.

OUR INCOME THIS MONTH IS $1,603.⁵⁰, AND OUR EXPENSES ARE $1,250.⁰⁰. THAT MEANS THAT OUR INCOME IS GREATER THAN OUR EXPENSES!

RIGHT! THIS MONTH WE HAVE MONEY LEFT OVER!

A family's financial situation is in trouble when its
income is less than its expenses. When the money
a family receives is not as much as the money it
spends, there will not be enough money for the
family to get what it needs and wants.

There are two reasons why a family's income is less than its expenses.

1. The income stays the same while the expenses increase.
2. The income decreases while the expenses stay the same.

There are several things that can cause a family's expenses to increase.

Inflation, or a general rise in prices, can increase a family's expenses. When inflation happens, everything a family needs or wants begins to cost more.

Changes in a family's needs or wants can cause its expenses to increase or decrease. If a family needs more or wants more, its expenses will be more.

There are several things that can cause a family's income to decrease.

If a family member's salary is cut, the family income will decrease. People's salaries decrease when they are paid less, or end when they lose their jobs.

If a family that has been receiving money from savings, investments, or gifts stops getting that money, the income will decrease.

If any of the following things happen to your family. . .

- inflation increases expenses,
- the family's wants or needs increase,
- salary is cut or a job is lost, or
- the family stops getting income from savings, investments, or gifts

. . .you may be sure that your parents will respond to most of your requests by saying. . .

When your parents tell you, "We can't afford it!" you may feel **disappointed**.

GEE WHiZ!
AM I DISAPPOINTED!
ALL I WANTED WAS A
LOUSY PAIR OF DUMB OLD
SNEAKERS. ALL THE
OTHER KIDS HAVE NEW
SHOES! BUT NO, NOT ME!
COMPLAIN
COMPLAIN
COMPLAIN...

Because you are disappointed, you may want to
complain.

When your parents tell you, "We can't afford it!"
you may feel **frustrated.**

Because you feel frustrated, you may want to **nag** and possibly **throw a tantrum**.

When your parents tell you, "We can't afford it!"
you may feel **cheated**.

Because you feel cheated, you may do anything to try to get your parents to buy you what you want. You may **threaten** your parents or **badger** them.

But complaining, nagging, threatening, or
badgering your parents will not help. These things
do nothing to increase a family's income. They do
nothing to decrease a family's expenses.

Complaining, nagging, threatening, or badgering only makes things worse. These things cause your parents to feel guilty, hurt, and angry. Such feelings may hinder your parents from doing what they need to do to solve the problem.

Don't hinder your parents. Help them! There are six things you can do to help your parents when the family finances are in trouble.

1. Be Understanding.

Try to understand what your parents are going through.

If you do this, your attitude will improve and
you will be able to give your parents the
encouragement and support they need in
order to solve the problem.

2. Be Helpful.

Take care of yourself. Clean up after yourself and help out around the house.

If you do these things, your parents can spend more time doing what they need to do to earn the money that is needed.

3. Be Careful, Not Wasteful.

Take care of your things and the things that belong to the family. Do not waste food or resources like gas, electricity, or water.

If you take care of things, money will not have to be spent on repairing or replacing them. If you are not wasteful, money will not be spent unnecessarily.

4. Stop Careless Spending.

Do not spend money on things that you do not need, like junk food, frivolous toys, games, or extra clothes. Do not insist on going places and doing things that cost money. Learn to entertain yourself without spending money.

If you stop spending money carelessly, there will be more money to spend on the things that are necessary.

5. Earn Some Money.

Look around your community. See if there is anything you can do to earn money.

The money you make from any job you get will provide you with money to buy things your family may not be able to afford. This will help your parents, as anything you buy is one less thing they have to buy.

6. Get Involved in Your Family's Finances.

Talk with your parents about your family's income and expenses. Find out about your family's financial situation and offer to help in any way you can.

This will make you part of the solution rather than part of the problem. You will most likely stop asking for things your parents cannot afford, and you will begin to do what you can to help them solve the family's problems.

There is a game that your family can play to help you understand your family's finances.

This is what you will need in order to play the game:

- play money (you can buy it or make it)
- a listing of your family's income (for one month)
- copies of your family's bills (for one month)

This is how you play the game:

- Count out enough play money to equal the family's total income for one month.
- Display the bills. Lay them out so that every bill is showing at the same time.
- Using the play money, count out the amount that is needed to pay each bill.
- Put the appropriate amount of play money with each bill.
- After all of the bills have been paid, count the money that is left, or add the bills that are still left to pay.

After you have played the game, discuss these questions with your parents:

- Is the income greater than the expenses?
- If it is, what should be done with the extra income?
- Are the expenses greater than the income?
- If they are, what should be done to take care of the additional expenses?
- What can be done to increase the income?
- What can be done to decrease the expenses?

45

Remember, no two families are the same. Every one is different. Since your family is not like any other family, you should not compare your family with others.

When you compare your family with other families, you may begin to compete with them. Competing with other families may take your attention away from your own family and keep you from working to solve your family's problems.

It may help you to remember that all families, no matter what their situations are, have things to be thankful for.

And all families, no matter who they are, have problems to solve.

Successful families are ones that are thankful for what they have and are committed to solving their problems.

Mutual support and love and understanding help to achieve this.

Your understanding and help can mean **THE END** of your parents' having to say, "We can't afford it!"